National Parks
Zion

TAMRA B. ORR

Children's Press®
An Imprint of Scholastic Inc.

Content Consultant
James Gramann, PhD
Professor, Department of Recreation, Park and Tourism Sciences
Texas A&M University, College Station, Texas

Library of Congress Cataloging-in-Publication Data
Names: Orr, Tamra, author.
Title: Zion / Tamra B. Orr.
Description: New York : Children's Press, an imprint of Scholastic Inc., 2018. | Series: A true book
  | Includes index.
Identifiers: LCCN 2017004666 | ISBN 9780531233979 (library binding) | ISBN 9780531240243 (pbk.)
Subjects: LCSH: Zion National Park (Utah)—Juvenile literature.
Classification: LCC F832.Z8 O77 2018 | DDC 979.2/48—dc23
LC record available at https://lccn.loc.gov/2017004666

SCHOLASTIC, CHILDREN'S PRESS, A TRUE BOOK™, and associated logos are trademarks and/or registered trademarks of Scholastic Inc., 557 Broadway, New York, NY 10012.
1 2 3 4 5 6 7 8 9 10 R 27 26 25 24 23 22 21 20 19 18

3 1907 00382 0734

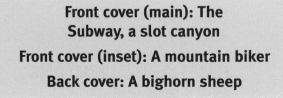

Front cover (main): The
Subway, a slot canyon
Front cover (inset): A mountain biker
Back cover: A bighorn sheep

★ Find the Truth!

Everything you are about to read is true *except* for one of the sentences on this page.

Which one is **TRUE**?

T or F   The Mormons were the first people to live in Zion.

T or F   Sunlight rarely reaches the bottom of Zion Canyon.

Find the answers in this book.

3

Contents

THE **BIG** TRUTH!

A mountain lion

The Virgin River

Hikers

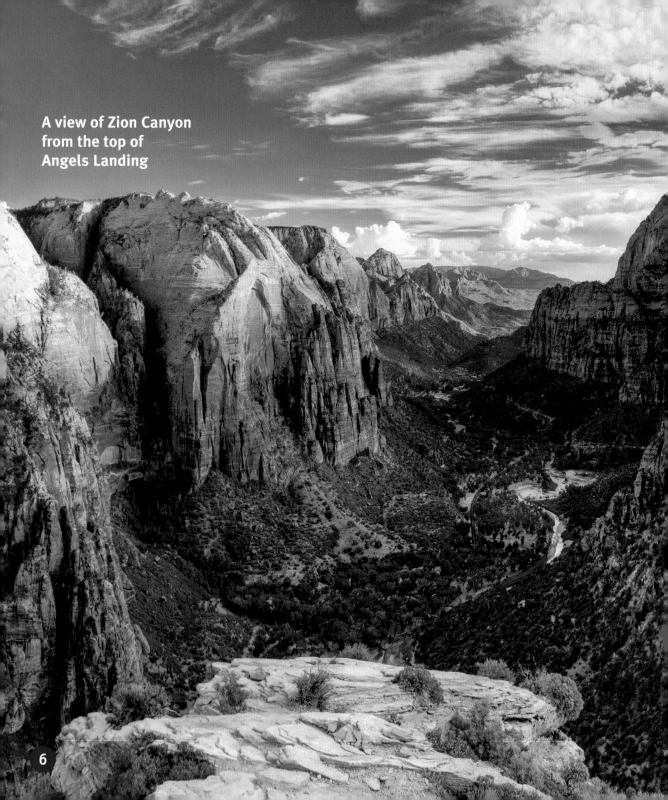

A view of Zion Canyon from the top of Angels Landing

CHAPTER 1

Finding Paradise

Looking at the colorful layers of the canyons of Zion National Park in southwestern Utah is like looking back across countless centuries. It is hard to imagine that these deep, shadowed canyons were once just flat land. They were transformed by millions of years of water and wind pushing, blowing, and changing everything in their path.

Zion's first name was Mukuntuweap, meaning "straight canyon."

★Zion National Park

Gradual Changes

Nature created one of the most beautiful places on Earth, but it happened very slowly. Water carried **sediment** to the area. It piled up, one layer on top of the next. The color changed based on what was in the sediments and where they came from. Over millions of years, these sediments hardened into rock. The force of the water flowing through the rocks shaped canyons. Constant wind formed huge sand dunes.

Timeline of Zion History

10,000 BCE
Humans first settle in what is now Utah.

1850s
European and non-Native American explorers arrive, including Mormons.

6th to 14th centuries CE
The Ancient Puebloans thrive in what is now Utah.

The First People

For a long time, no one was there to witness these changes. The first humans arrived 12,000 years ago. Imagine sneaking through southern Utah that long ago. You might be armed with a spear, chasing a mammoth or giant sloth! Early hunters pursued these huge animals here. The hunters were followed by a culture of basket weavers. Later, the Ancient Puebloans populated Zion. They were excellent farmers and thrived for about 800 years.

1919
Zion is named a U.S. national park.

1927–1930
The Zion-Mount Carmel Highway is built.

2000
A shuttle system to the park is added for visitors.

Rapid Changes

In the 1800s, many explorers came to Utah. Some were Mormons, who are part of a religious group called the Church of Jesus Christ of Latter-day Saints. They named the area Zion, a Hebrew word associated with Jerusalem and with paradise. People shared descriptions and images of this land's unique beauty.

In 1919, the U.S. government declared Zion a national park. But the park was hard to reach. To fix this, workers constructed the Zion-Mount Carmel Highway over three years. Workers blasted through thousands of feet of solid sandstone. They dug a 1-mile (1.6 kilometers) tunnel. Now, the world could visit!

VIEW FROM ONE OF THE GALLERIES IN TUNNEL ON ZION – MT. CARMEL HIGHWAY

National Park Fact File

A national park is land that is protected by the federal government. It is a place of importance to the United States because of its beauty, history, or value to scientists. The U.S. Congress creates a national park by passing a law. Here are some key facts about Zion National Park.

Zion National Park	
Location	Southwest Utah
Year established	1919
Size	229 square miles (593 sq km)
Average number of visitors each year	4.2 million
Height of the tallest mountain	8,726 feet (2,660 m), Horse Ranch Mountain
Most dangerous hiking trail	Angels Landing

The Great White Throne is difficult to climb.

t

o see
of the
e Great
named
nolith,
et
tone.
iful

est.

Cliffs and a Checkerboard

The same minister named the Court of the **Patriarchs**. Individually, the sandstone cliffs are known as Abraham, Isaac, and Jacob, the patriarchs of the Bible. Found on the canyon's west side, their peaks reach nearly 7,000 feet (2,134 m).

Another unusual site is the Checkerboard Mesa. A mesa is a steep, flat-topped hill. Lines crisscross the side of the mesa along the Zion-Mount Carmel highway. It looks like a huge checkerboard.

The long grooves in the Checkerboard Mesa make it easily recognizable.

Kolob Arch is more difficult to reach than other arches in the park, but the view is worth the trip.

Under the Arch

Zion National Park features many natural stone arches. These unique structures were created from millions of years of **erosion** and temperature changes. The Kolob Arch is the longest arch in the park and the third longest in the world. It stretches almost 288 feet (88 m) across and is a popular place for people to hike. It is sometimes hard to see, as it blends in with the gold, brown, and orange in the surrounding cliff sides.

Hikers hold onto chains as they cross the narrow Leap of Faith portion of the route up Angels Landing.

Watch Your Step!

Many people who come to Zion are eager to hike through it. One of the most incredible—but also dangerous—hikes in the park leads to Angels Landing. The path is narrow, with very sharp drop-offs on either side. The peak is 5,790 feet (1,765 m) high. Hikers claim the view of the canyon and the Virgin River far, far below is definitely worth the challenging climb.

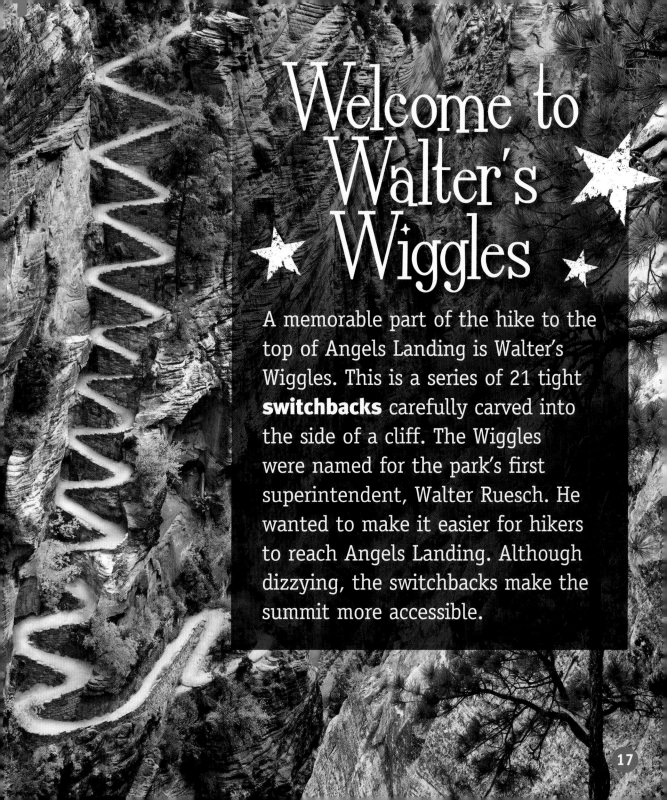

Welcome to Walter's Wiggles

A memorable part of the hike to the top of Angels Landing is Walter's Wiggles. This is a series of 21 tight **switchbacks** carefully carved into the side of a cliff. The Wiggles were named for the park's first superintendent, Walter Ruesch. He wanted to make it easier for hikers to reach Angels Landing. Although dizzying, the switchbacks make the summit more accessible.

On Board for Adventure

Adventurous visitors who plan ahead may reserve permits for Zion's Subway. The Subway is not an underground train! It's a trail that goes through a tube-like canyon. Hikers choose from two routes. One is a 9-mile (14.5 km) trek across creeks and over boulders, all in limited light. The other path is slightly longer. Hikers rappel, or descend using a rope, down cliffs. They also swim through frigid pools before they climb out—straight uphill!

With its wide, rounded bottom and much narrower top opening, the Subway is a lot like a tunnel.

Get Your Feet Wet

One of Zion's most popular hikes is through the Narrows. This **gorge**, as its name suggests, is narrow, with walls up to 1,000 feet (305 m) high. A hike through the Narrows means getting wet, since a portion of it requires crossing the Virgin River.

Depending on the time of year and the weather, the water may be up to your knees—or all the way to your chest. Flash floods are always a concern, especially in spring and summer. (For more information on flash floods, see page 37.)

Hikers wade through water in the Narrows.

CHAPTER 3

From Common to Endangered

Although humans no longer live in Zion, the park is home to many other creatures. Zion teems with wildlife, from common and familiar animals to **endangered** and unusual ones—as well as everything in between. Bighorn sheep scramble over the rocky slopes of the park's eastern side. Wild turkeys wander in Zion Canyon, while beavers build along the Virgin River.

Human activity wiped out bighorn sheep from Zion. Now humans have helped restore them.

In the Sky

Hundreds of bird species live in Zion. Hummingbirds flit from one cottonwood tree to the next. Black ravens croak overhead, searching for berries and seeds. Endangered birds also live safely inside the park's protected borders. The peregrine falcon nests here. The California condor, with its almost 10-foot (3 m) wingspan, soars past. The Mexican spotted owl roosts in trees, hunting at night like a silent ghost.

Many condors bear tags on their wings, placed there by researchers.

The collared lizard is named for the black stripes at its neck.

On the Ground

Scattered throughout Zion are hundreds of mammals, reptiles, and amphibians. Rock squirrels scamper over and under rocks. Mule deer stroll through Zion Canyon, using their 9-inch (23-centimeter) ears to carry heat away from their bodies. Mountain lions prowl at night, along with ringtail cats and coyotes. Sixteen types of lizards live here, including the Great Basin collared lizard. When it stands on its hind legs, it is almost 14 inches (36 cm) tall!

Canyon tree frogs cling to rock near a pond along Pine Creek.

In the Water

Different types of frogs and toads are found near waterways in Zion. The canyon tree frog has suction cups on each toe that help it climb. Its coloring keeps it **camouflaged** among the rocks. The Woodhouse's toad is active when water is available, but burrows underground when the water runs out. It stays there until the next rainfall. The Virgin River is full of fish with names like flannelmouth sucker and spinedace.

Tiny—and Huge

It is not often that a creature is known for being tiny and huge at the same time. But the Zion snail is! As snails go, it is one of the smallest in the world. It measures less than 0.8 inches (2 cm) long. As tiny as it is, however, the Zion snail's foot, when compared to the size of the rest of its body, is the biggest in the world!

This tiny creature is found only in Zion.

National Parks Field Guide: Zion

Here are just a few of the animals that live in Zion National Park.

Peregrine falcon

Scientific name: *Falco peregrinus*

Habitat: Throughout the park

Diet: Birds such as starlings, pigeons, and doves

Fact: This falcon can capture prey in flight by diving at up to 200 miles (322 km) per hour!

Southwestern willow flycatcher

Scientific name: *Empidonax traillii extimus*

Habitat: Near swamps, rivers, and other wetlands

Diet: Insects

Fact: This bird has been listed as endangered since 1995.

Desert tortoise

Scientific name: *Gopherus agassizii*

Habitat: Desert areas

Diet: Grasses, herbs, cacti, and flowers

Fact: These tortoises, which burrow deep underground during the hottest months, live about 50 years.

Mountain lion

Scientific name: *Puma concolor*

Habitat: Forest and mountainous regions

Diet: Mule deer, bighorn sheep

Fact: Born blind, baby mountain lions are on their own by six months of age.

North American porcupine

Scientific name: *Erethion dorsatum*

Habitat: Desert and forest areas

Diet: Plants, tree bark, conifer needles

Fact: Zion's porcupines hide in hollow or downed trees and come out only at night.

Speckled dace

Scientific name: *Rhinichthys osculus*

Habitat: Cool to warm creeks, rivers, and lakes

Diet: Insects and algae

Fact: This fish is related to minnows and is endangered in some states.

Ecosystems and Elevations

Zion National Park truly has a little of everything when it comes to weather and geology. Zion Canyon is so deep that it is rare for sunlight to reach the bottom. In other parts of the park, it seems like the mountains are trying to make up for the deep canyons. Peaks soar thousands of feet up, as if reaching for the sun.

Some wildflowers bloom and produce seeds very quickly while the spring rains last.

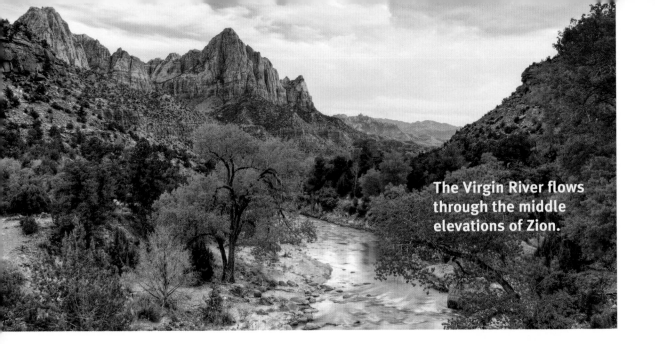

The Virgin River flows through the middle elevations of Zion.

Elevation Is Key

Because of the huge differences in **elevation**, what grows in Zion National Park often differs dramatically from one spot to another. It all depends on a complex combination of seasons, temperatures, and the amount of **precipitation** and sunshine each area receives. Higher elevations mean colder temperatures and snow. Lower elevations mean hot, dry, desertlike conditions. In between, near the Virgin River, trees, wildflowers, and other plants are thick and colorful.

Going Down

At the lowest elevation, Zion's heat is often intense. **Drought** is common. Hardy grasses and shrubs grow here. Various types of cactus are also found, including purple torch, prickly pear, and cholla. Many of these have bright flowers that bloom for a brief time.

Wildflowers such as the desert marigold and the slickrock paintbrush bloom in the spring. Their time is short, but their colors are incredible.

Bright pink flowers bloom among the sharp spines of a prickly pear cactus.

Going Up

The middle elevation of Zion features forests full of juniper and other tough evergreens. Juniper roots push through cracks in the sandstone in search of water. Ponderosa pines, fir, and aspen grow higher up. Along the Virgin River's banks, cottonwoods provide welcome shade in the summer and golden leaves in the fall.

Flowers in higher elevations include the golden columbine and the shooting star. Ferns and mosses add to the greenery. All these plants grow out of the crevices in rocks and cliffsides, creating beautiful hanging gardens.

High Elevations

Flowers, ferns, and mosses create "hanging gardens" in the crevices of the higher elevations.

Shooting star

Ferns and mosses

Middle Elevations

Tough evergreens and some deciduous (non-evergreen) trees grow in the middle elevations.

Cottonwood

Juniper

Low Elevations

Cacti grow in the low elevations, along with wildflowers that bloom in spring.

Cholla

Slickrock paintbrush

A park ranger talks with a visitor in the Big Bend area.

CHAPTER 5

A Changing Landscape

There is no doubt that Zion National Park is one of the most beautiful parks in the country. The people who work at the park want to make sure it stays that way. There are several threats to Zion, and it is important that the park be protected for the future as much as possible.

 Zion is busiest between March through October.

Threats From Nature

One of the biggest threats in the park is a natural one: flash floods. Flash floods happen during thunderstorms, when a great deal of rain falls suddenly in the area. Water levels in low elevations such as the Narrows rise dangerously in seconds. Many of the area's plants have evolved to withstand or recover from these floods, but the quickly rising waters pose a serious risk to hikers. Although visitors are warned, there is no way to contact them if weather conditions suddenly worsen.

During flash floods, search-and-rescue workers provide aid to endangered hikers at great personal risk.

Flood Awareness

Whenever you're in low elevations in Zion, watch and listen for these signs of a possible flash flood. This is particularly important in narrow canyon areas. If you notice any of these signs, move to higher ground immediately.

Watch

- Clouds gathering in the sky
- Water changing suddenly from clear to cloudy
- Water level rising or the current becoming stronger
- Debris floating in the water

Listen

- Thunder
- Increasing roar of water

Unfortunately not all visitors clean up after themselves, leaving park workers to pick up trash.

Threats From People

Most of the danger to Zion comes from humans. The millions of visitors who come to the park each year wear down trails and bother plants and animals. Some leave litter. Visitors also play a part in protecting the park. People are encouraged to have "zero impact" on the park by staying on marked trails, properly disposing of trash, and not bothering or damaging plants and animals.

Climate change is another concern. A small change in overall temperatures can have major effects in places like Zion. The park is fighting this by switching to "climate friendly" energy sources such as solar power, and by reducing electricity use.

Zion National Park is a place of unique beauty and history. We must work together to make sure it remains this way for many years to come! ★

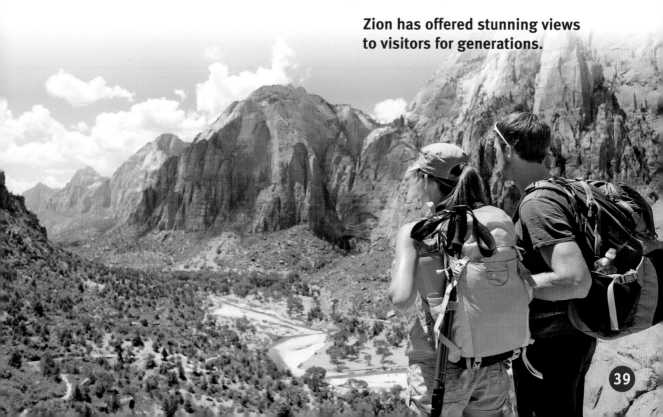

Zion has offered stunning views to visitors for generations.

Map Mystery

One of the most popular hikes in Zion is also a dangerous one. What is its name? Follow the directions below to find the answer.

Directions

1. Start at the East Entrance on the Zion-Mount Carmel Highway.

2. Head west along the highway to the Zion Human History Museum.

3. Hike north to the Grotto, where you can stop for a picnic.

4. You're almost there! Cross the river to the West Rim Trail and follow the trail uphill to the north. (Be careful!)

5. Find the top, where winged creatures are supposed to be able to land, and you will solve the mystery.

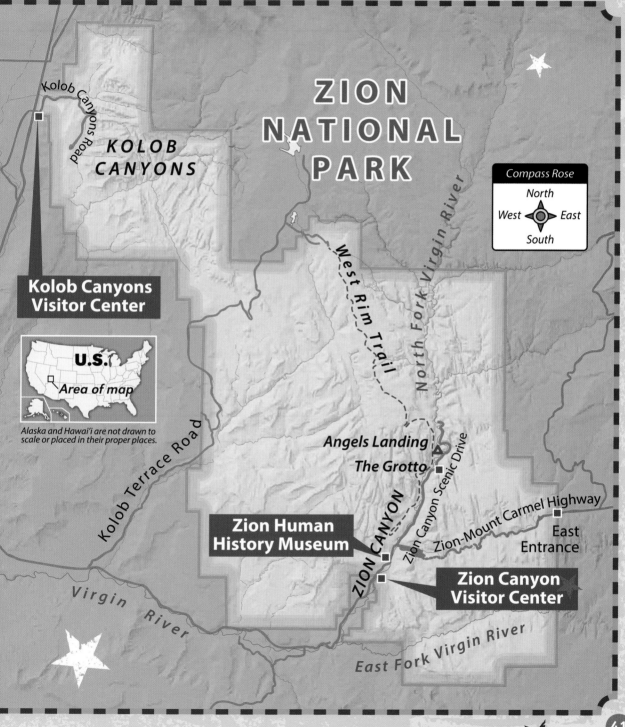

ZION NATIONAL PARK

KOLOB CANYONS

Kolob Canyons Road

Kolob Canyons Visitor Center

U.S.

Area of map

Alaska and Hawai'i are not drawn to scale or placed in their proper places.

Compass Rose

North

West • East

South

West Rim Trail

North Fork Virgin River

Kolob Terrace Road

Angels Landing

The Grotto

ZION CANYON

Zion Canyon Scenic Drive

Zion Human History Museum

Zion Canyon Visitor Center

Zion-Mount Carmel Highway

East Entrance

Virgin River

East Fork Virgin River

Be an Animal Tracker!

If you're ever in Zion National Park, keep an eye out for these animal tracks. They'll help you know which animals are in the area.

Bighorn sheep
Hoof length: 3.5 inches (9 cm)

Mountain lion
Paw length: 3 inches (8 cm)

North American porcupine

Paw length: 3.5 to 5 inches
(9 to 13 cm)

Mule deer

Hoof length: 3 inches (8 cm)

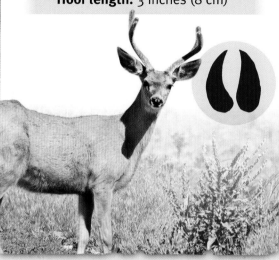

Wild turkey

Foot length: 4 inches (10 cm)

Beaver

Front paw length: 3 inches (8 cm)

True Statistics

Year tourists first visited Zion by car: 1917

Number of plant species that grow in Zion National Park but nowhere else in Utah: 8

Highest elevation in the park: 8,726 ft. (2,660 m), at Horse Ranch Mountain

Lowest elevation in the park: 3,666 ft. (1,117 m), at Coal Pits Wash

Number of lightning-caused fires in the park between 1965 and 2011: 443

Number of visitors in 1920: 3,692

Average number of yearly visitors today: 4.2 million

Did you find the truth?

F The Mormons were the first people to live in Zion.

T Sunlight rarely reaches the bottom of Zion Canyon.

Resources

Books

Flynn, Sarah Wassner, and Julie Beer. *National Parks Guide U.S.A.*
Washington, DC: National Geographic, 2016.

Marsted, Melissa. *Buzzy and the Red Rock Canyons: Utah's National
Park*s. Park City, UT: Lucky Penny Press, 2016.

McHugh, Erin. *National Parks: A Kid's Guide to America's Parks,
Monuments, and Landmarks*. New York: Black Dog & Leventhal
Publishers, 2012.

Weintraub, Eileen. *Secrets of the National Parks: Weird and Wonderful
Facts About America's Natural Wonders*. New York: Sterling Children's
Books, 2016.

**Visit this Scholastic website for more
information on Zion National Park:**
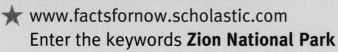 www.factsfornow.scholastic.com
Enter the keywords **Zion National Park**

Important Words

camouflaged (KAM-uh-flahzhd) colored, shaped, or otherwise disguised to look like one's surroundings

drought (DROUT) a long period without rain

elevation (el-uh-VAY-shuhn) the height above sea level

endangered (en-DAYN-jurd) at risk of becoming extinct, usually because of human activity

erosion (i-ROH-zhuhn) the wearing away of something by water or wind

gorge (GORJ) a deep valley or ravine

monolith (MAH-nuh-lith) a very large, usually tall and narrow stone

patriarchs (PAY-tree-ahrks) male heads of a family, group, or tribe

precipitation (prih-sip-uh-TAY-shuhn) the falling of water from the sky in the form of rain, sleet, hail, or snow

sediment (SED-uh-muhnt) rock, sand, or dirt that has been carried to a place by water, wind, or a glacier

switchbacks (SWICH-baks) roads or trails with many sharp turns that climb a steep hill

Index

Page numbers in **bold** indicate illustrations.

About the Author

Tamra Orr is the author of hundreds of books for readers of all ages. She has a degree in English and secondary education from Ball State University in Indiana, and now lives in the Pacific Northwest. She is the mother of four children and loves to spend her free time reading, writing, and going camping. When she visited Zion National Park, she was astonished at how beautiful it is.